reinvent
yourself

FIONA HARROLD

reinvent
yourself

7 steps to a
fresh new you

PIATKUS

Visit the Piatkus website!

Piatkus publishes a wide range of bestselling fiction and
non-fiction, including books on health, mind, body & spirit,
sex, self-help, cookery, biography and the paranormal.

If you want to:
- read descriptions of our popular titles
- buy our books over the Internet
- take advantage of our special offers
- enter our monthly competition
- learn more about your favourite Piatkus authors

VISIT OUR WEBSITE AT: www.piatkus.co.uk

Copyright © 2004 by Fiona Harrold

First published in 2004 by
Piatkus Books Ltd
5 Windmill Street
London W1T 2JA
e-mail: info@piatkus.co.uk

The moral right of the author has been asserted

*A catalogue record for this book is available
from the British Library*

ISBN 0 7499 2483 7

Text design by Briony Chappell
Edited by Krystyna Mayer

This book has been printed on paper manufactured
with respect for the environment using wood from
managed sustainable resources.

Data manipulation by
Action Publishing Technology, Gloucester
Printed and bound in Hong Kong by
Everbest Printing Co. Ltd.

FOR

Gutsy, get-up-and-go, good-hearted people everywhere.

Thanks to Alan Brooke for his initial push and constant enthusiasm for *Reinvent Yourself* and his subtle, always spot-on editing. Respect to the incomparable Judy Piatkus who knows all about reinvention, having masterminded her own 25 years ago to become the founder of Piatkus Books. And thanks to everyone involved with the production of *Reinvent Yourself* at Piatkus, from start to finish, to getting it onto the shelves of a good bookshop near you! Thanks a million.

Contents

1

Who are you now?

**It is never too late to be what
you might have been.**

GEORGE ELIOT

This is one of the most thrilling and important sentences you'll ever read. Memorise it. Think about it. Savour it. Digest it. Drop it deep into your psyche. Let this profound truth shape your life from this day forth. It contains within it all you ever need to know to stay fresh in life, to keep yourself young, open to life and to your own terrific, unlimited potential.

Mary Ann Evans said this over 150 years ago. She knew all about reinvention even then, in Victorian England, when she had to appear to be a man, George Eliot, in order to get her wonderful novels published. She fulfilled her childhood dream of writing fiction at the age of thirty-seven, when her first novel was published. Her finest work, *Middlemarch*, was published in 1871 when she was fifty-two – so she also knew about not giving up on herself. Thankfully, things have changed since then, but the urge to be the best that we can and being inventive along the way is perennial, as relevant today as it was then.

You are an ambitious person. You have an innate desire to be someone, to live a terrific life, make it all work, no regrets. I know this because you're here reading this right now, and because I've never met a single person who didn't fit this description. Certainly, I've met people who've given up on themselves, on life, who're resigned and are waiting to be rescued by fate, God, someone or something. Sometimes the something is death.

> **You have an innate desire to be someone.**

I've met lots of people who think life has been unfair to them, resenting other people's success instead of concentrating on their own. Overwhelming self-doubt and lack of confidence can prevent people from ever starting.

I've met other people whose politics and perspective simply don't allow them to have it all, to be happy and love life, because they're convinced they have to be miserable to change the world, or that perhaps they just don't deserve to be happy and have a wonderful life. I should know because I used to be one of these people! Whatever the situation, underneath it all is the same human desire to live a good life, to make it all work and to be the best *you* that you could possibly be. The fact that people suppress, thwart and deny that fundamental urge is another matter.

George Eliot had an incredible urge for life, a huge appetite to fulfil her potential and live a life of her own design. She earned her own living at a time when a good marriage was the route offered to and expected of ladies. She moved from the provincial Midlands of England to a place of her own in London's Chelsea. She was considered plain by conventional standards, yet had a racy love life, causing a scandal by living with a married man, her 'spiritual' husband for many years. After his death she married a man twenty years her junior, forty years old to her sixty. Thought by many to be rather serious, her regular salons were the hub of intellectual, Bohemian society at the time.

I want that same vibrancy and exuberance for you. I want you to feel excited about your life, yourself and what lies ahead for you. It doesn't matter in the slightest if you've become a little tired, even worn out. Never mind how jaded or downright cynical you may sometimes feel. In fact, everyone needs to take a good look at themselves now and then just to check that they're still happy with the person they've become or are turning into, and that life's challenges haven't left their mark in a negative way.

Nearly twenty years ago I would have been unrecognisable as the person I am now. After studying at university in Ireland, I came to London to live a little and 'find' myself. I worked as a waitress in a cocktail bar and sang with the band Nocturnal Emissions – well, it was London in the Eighties! I became involved with political campaigns including Ken Livingstone's Fair Fares initiative, stopping cruise missiles at Greenham Common, supporting the miners' strike of 1984 and writing for a local community newspaper.

This was a heady time, and ultimately disappointing and dispiriting for me. I didn't feel that I had succeeded in any of my endeavours, all of which I cared about deeply in that unconditional, youthful and unguarded way. I felt powerless and desperate, worn out and unable to make a difference to the world. I became more extreme in my views, moved into a squat and immersed myself totally in a counter-culture lifestyle. I also felt increasingly exhausted.

As my enthusiasm and optimism declined, so did my health. Nearly three stone heavier than I am now, I knew I was at rock bottom. Significantly, I had come to fear and dislike the person I had become. All my worst traits had become exaggerated and I had made no effort to control them. I was ferociously intolerant, emphatically dogmatic, thoroughly arrogant, short-tempered, rude and humourless. My companions loved me for it. It was entertaining for them, but exhausting for me. I felt poisoned by my own venom, the hatred that I regularly stoked up to inflame my indignation at all the wrongs and injustices in the world. Promoting peace was killing me.

Saving me became my mission. I called a truce with the world and pulled back to rethink my position. I was about to embark on the biggest reinvention of my life, mind, body, soul and spirit. I knew I was fighting for my life this time. Everything had to change – friends, where I lived and my entire outlook, attitude and appearance. Nothing could stay the same.

I transformed myself on the inside and on the outside. I tried every alternative therapy and treatment to restore my energy. I adored massage and began to train in it myself. I discovered teachers and writers such as Louise Hay, Wayne Dyer and Sondra Ray. I found a fabulous woman in London, Fiona Shaw, who worked tirelessly to open my mind again to enjoying life, and to not feeling guilty about making my life work. I had to relearn how to be a natural optimist again.

I apprenticed myself to Fiona to learn the tools of her trade. For eighteen months I was happy to clean her treatment rooms, make tea for her workshop groups – to do absolutely anything in return for her expert tuition. I will always be grateful to her, as I must have been one of her most difficult and stubborn clients!

I took every personal development course, seminar and workshop going, from the Loving Relationships

Training to the Forum. I adored the big American ones; the more confrontational the better! Ironically, one of the therapies I was attracted to was rebirthing, which involved identifying your core thoughts and beliefs from birth and replacing the negative ones with more positive ones.

I lost weight and got slim, moved to a gorgeous house, got a cat and opened up a massage and self-esteem consultancy – the term coaching wasn't in our vocabulary then as it is now, but that's what I was doing. My mentor, Fiona Shaw, fell in love with the handsome Italian who owned the restaurant below her treatment rooms and moved to Sicily, handing over her practice to me. A new chapter in my life began. I'd come a long, long way from sleeping on the floor of a Brixton squat.

You may not need to carry out such an extreme transformation, but whatever changes you feel motivated to make, a new chapter of your life is about to begin. Your reinvention may be prompted by a defining event: a divorce, an illness, a wake-up call of sorts. Or you may have outgrown a part of your life and need to open it up for more movement. Sometimes life just needs a shake-up to prevent it from going stale. Keeping fresh requires regular checks. Stagnation can creep up and take the shine off any area of your life – your job, your relationship, your health, your appearance.

Whatever your motivation, you are going to take a good look at *you*, who you're turning into and, most importantly, who you want to be. The fact that you're reading this book tells you that your appetite for life has not dulled. It may benefit from some awakening and stimulating, but that's what I'm going to work on with you over the days and weeks ahead.

Over the years I've worked successfully with hundreds of people who needed to renew their enthusiasm for life. Thousands of individuals all over the world have made *Reinvent Yourself* my most popular online course. On the basis of other people's success and my own personal experience, I can assure you that you can be the person you've always wanted to be.

I will coach you to become that person. I will treat you as an important private client who is perfectly well – mentally and emotionally robust. I will have the highest expectations for you while ensuring that you are entirely grounded and practical about the work that you may have to do to refine yourself and take yourself to the next level in your life. I want you to succeed and I know every pitfall that you may stumble into, so you can rely on me to point these out; I've walked this path many times before.

For your part, I ask that you be totally honest with yourself in your self-appraisal and do the work that I ask you to do, both while you are reading a chapter and at the end of it. You'll be inspired by the real-life examples I'll give you of great reinventers, some well-known public figures, others private clients. I'll give you tools, tips and techniques to follow that work. Your success, however, is down to you. No matter how great the coach or trainer, only you can do the actual work. It's your re-invention. It's down to you.

Before I turn the spotlight on you and get to work, I need to ensure that you understand an essential rule of successful transformation. It's this: enjoying what you have in the now is one of life's gifts – and challenges.

> **Enjoying what you have in the now is one of life's gifts – and challenges.**

Don't make life intolerable for yourself in the present as you shape your future. Appreciation and understanding of where you are right now is crucial. Resist the temptation and tendency of many overly eager self-improvers to undervalue, even loathe yourself right now. Do not suspend liking yourself until you're someone else.

I have come across people who have been 'working on' themselves – improving themselves – for twenty years and more, attending seminars, reading every self-help book that was ever written. Such people are perpetually dissatisfied, searching for an ever-elusive perfection. They are trading their self-esteem for the Holy Grail of self-improvement. Refuse to repeat their mistake of only seeing what's missing, what you lack, what you need to have, be and do in the future.

Do not underestimate how damaging and destructive such an attitude is to the spirit. By withholding appreciation and self-respect from themselves in the present, these people assume they are motivating themselves to push forward. This is nonsense. Beating yourself up is not an effective way to build morale and motivation. By the time you reach your destination you will probably have lost the knack of liking yourself altogether, and already be fixated on the next set of goals. I have seen this pattern many times, and it always results in chronically low self-esteem and a lack of pleasure in yourself and your achievements. Training yourself to see only what's missing means that whatever you achieve, you will only ever see what's missing.

> **Training yourself to see only what's missing means that whatever you achieve, you will only ever see what's missing.**

Thankfully, this will not be the case for you.

This is not what true reinvention is about. The reinvention I have in mind for you does not require you to be another person. It requires you to be the best version of you. I want you to be the *you* that you know you could be, that you intrinsically know you are, at your most polished, powerful and perfected, free from unwanted hold-you-back personality traits or out-of-date ideas about who you arc or could be.

Right now, pat yourself on the back for being brave and

bright enough to challenge yourself, to reflect honestly and enquire within and make any changes you see fit to make. Remember, there doesn't have to be anything really wrong with you or your life to run this check. You're looking to upscale, trade up and ensure you're making the most of your potential; that you are on the right track to live a life you love. This is the mark of an achiever, an alert, switched-on person. The objective here is to refine and polish you, to prune, trim, tone and uplift you. But do not turn this into an exercise in self-loathing. This would only hamper your momentum, determination and enthusiasm. I admire you enormously for being here, engaged in this enquiry. Ensure you feel the same way. Let's press on.

➤ *Look at You*

Life can take it out of you. It's easy to get coated with layers of resignation, cynicism, self-doubt and pessimism. This results in a dampening of your spirit, vibrancy and optimism, a shutting down of what's possible for you, for your life. I want to slough off those layers, so that you see yourself anew and take a fresh look at you. Before we even think of bringing new qualities, attitudes or actions to you, we need to take stock and appreciate what you're entirely happy with and proud of right now.

The trick is to decide to like yourself now *and* in the future. The best fuel you can use to drive yourself onwards is the healthy desire to do well by yourself: to feel that you owe it to yourself to make the most of yourself, that nothing and no one will deprive you of being the person you want to be, least of all yourself. And life is far too short to make it more diffi-cult than it need be. Give it your best shot. Get onside.

➤ *Reconcile the Past*

Moving forwards requires you to reconcile the past. It does not require you to bury the past or deny your history. A person of substance always has a past. This is what gives you your edge, your depth and wisdom. You may not want to repeat the past but it is essential that you put it into perspective so that you see yourself in the most productive and powerful way. It's essential to check that you're not carrying forwards any old regrets or resentments. Otherwise you could find yourself being so caught up with the past that your preoccupation binds you to it.

Your aim is to be free and freed up to concentrate fully on the present and future: neither wistfully clinging on to the past nor running scared from it. Making peace with the past prevents it from clouding your present or dictating your future.

> **Your aim is to be free and freed up to concentrate fully on the present and future.**

I also want to ensure that you are extracting full value from all your past experiences, regretting absolutely nothing as you appreciate how they have all helped make you the robust, resilient person you are today. I worked with a client recently to do just this.

Jennifer was an up-and-coming young actress who was about to take up a part in a popular British television series. This was her big break. Her enthusiasm was dampened by her fear of her past being exposed on the front pages of a tabloid newspaper.

In her early twenties Jennifer had attracted boyfriends who were violent and abusive. She felt ashamed and angry with herself for allowing this to happen. She loathed herself for having been so 'weak'. She was terrified that she would be exposed as a fool. She was also sure that she had resisted success because of the inevitable publicity it would bring.

I coached Jennifer to see the actual truth of that time: to see that her youth and inexperience had led her to attract and stay with these strong, domineering individuals. Her self-esteem was crushed and she had very little support around her at the time. She was no fool and made her escape when she felt able to. I also pointed out that the despair that Jennifer had felt must have given her an edge as an actor, and that she had a great strength and air of self-assurance as a direct consequence of coming through all that turmoil. She even had the look of someone with a past, and having a little mystery about you is no bad thing!

I drew Jennifer's attention to the fact that she had successfully broken free of this pattern by having attracted a terrific, respectful and adoring boyfriend in the present. With regard to tabloid exposure, she had done nothing to be ashamed of and would discuss her interesting past with a sympathetic journalist in her own time.

Jennifer was immediately able to see herself and her past in a different light, and actually felt quite compassionate towards herself in a way that she never had. This part of her past lost the hold it had had on her for many years. She began to appreciate how her experiences, however gruesome they may at times have been, actually set her apart and gave her a great depth that she wouldn't have had otherwise. She was no lightweight and had a strength that left her feeling able to handle anything life could throw at her.

➤ *Look Within*

Truly successful, enduring reinvention comes from digging deep into yourself and pulling out old beliefs and attitudes that restrict you and prevent you from fulfilling your potential, living the life you want to live and being the person you feel you genuinely are.

> **Truly successful, enduring reinvention comes from digging deep into yourself and pulling out old beliefs and attitudes that restrict you.**

Take a look at yourself. What do you see? Who are you now? Are you entirely happy with what you've become? It would be very easy to answer questions like these if we were talking about your body. You could tell me instantly whether you had 'let yourself go', were not at your best or had neglected yourself. But we're looking at the *person* you've become and are turning into. We're talking character and personality. That's more unusual. It's a fascinating and important conversation to have.

You could slip into being someone you wouldn't find attractive or interesting without even noticing. You could wake up some morning and not recognise the person in your own bed – you!

➤ *Who Are You?*

The question, 'Who am I?' is the one to ponder. Be absolutely clear. This is not a final, fixed state of affairs. We just need some answers to get clear on our work ahead. In the next few weeks you're going to experiment – try on some new traits, attitudes and airs. Don't even think about genes. They're such a small part of the picture. Don't let them get in the way of you grooming yourself to your own polished perfection, of your own making, self-styled to your own personal prescription.

THE WORK

1. Have an Attitude Audit

List the attitudes, traits and demeanour that no longer work for you. What do you need to throw off, walk away from, leave behind? For example, you could ➤

➤ have taken on a disgruntled, disaffected look that you wear without even noticing. It just got stuck. You forgot to take it off one evening and it's been there ever since. Are there traits that have crept into your outlook that you find distasteful? Root them out. Get them on paper. Look very closely at yourself. Identify what you don't want to carry forwards. Monitor your behaviour and what you're projecting about yourself. Watch yourself in action and take control. Rein in the attitudes that you don't want to be a part of you.

2. Admire Yourself Now

Make a list headed, 'Ten great qualities I admire about myself' and another list, 'Ten achievements of mine I am proud of'. Keep these lists open and add to them as more qualities and achievements occur to you. This is the foundation you need to build on, a secure footing from which you can work and sculpt from.

Demonstrate admiration for yourself. Soak in a glorious evening bath. Switch off and tune in to you. Revel in the comfort of knowing that you're moving on up, taking yourself in hand, ready to challenge yourself and do what it takes to be *more* brilliant. ➤

3. Grasp the Past

Making peace with the past doesn't have to take years of therapy, which could even keep you more stuck there. Grasp the lessons, and get to grips with moving on. It all begins and ends with an attitude shift on your part.

Ask yourself these questions: Who do I still blame/resent/need to forgive from the past. List the names and what you are holding against them. Don't neglect to include your own name here! Forgiveness will set you free and dissolve the ties that may pull you back to the past. Even a *willingness* to forgive will begin to unglue you from your attachment. Write this down: 'I am now ready to forgive [name/myself] for whatever.' Now write this down: 'The lessons I am taking from this experience are . . .'

The past is over. That was then. It's now and for ever that's important.

4. Make Space

Preparing for 'a fresh new you' requires action on all levels. Your home and your wardrobe need scrutiny. Take two hours to clear out old, worn-out or ➤

➤ redundant clothes and belongings. Give away gen-
erously, knowing that you're making room for something more fitting or just some clear space.

5. Get Excited!

Grasp the fact that you've embarked on a hugely
important and fascinating project – 'The Rebranding of
You'. If Gucci, Burberry, Prada and Chloe can do it, you
certainly can! Seriously, we're looking at a makeover
from the inside out. It's for real. You've taken the first
steps. You're here. You know what you've got to do. In
the next chapter we'll get clear on *who you want to be*.

**Moral: It's not where you've come from that
counts. It's where you're going.**

2

Who do you want to be?

Life's not about finding yourself. Life is about creating yourself.

GEORGE BERNARD SHAW

There are those who say that environment creates personality and character, while others believe you are born with your character intact, that character is destiny, that it determines the roads you take, the life you ultimately lead. Does biology decide fate? Is our destiny decided by where we are born in the sibling pecking order? Is the eldest child always most likely to be successful, the youngest child wild and the middle child the peace-maker? Are we purely the products of our parents' beliefs?

What I do know is that character shapes destiny and fate cannot override free will. Personality and character are paramount, and ultimately it is our *response* to our environment that shapes our lives. Once the deck of cards is split, you are the one dealing. It's always in your hand.

We are not victims of circumstances. It's not life that makes us. It's what we make of life. We arrive in the world with a personality, a distinct character. But what we do with it, how we develop ourselves, is entirely in our hands. When you think about it, life's just one great long self-improvement exercise, a non-stop march towards ever-greater refinement and poise. You just never stop evolving. You're a work in progress, a masterpiece of your own making. Who knows how great you could really be? The potential is untold. There's just no end to how good you could be.

> ### It's not life that makes us. It's what we make of life.

Do women have to turn into their mothers and men into their fathers? Do your genes dictate your future, or can you really choose who you want to be? In the nature versus nurture debate, adopted children have something to teach us. In a recent feature in British *Elle* the journalist Sophie Davies, herself adopted, said, 'Being adopted allows you to choose who you want to be, and shuffle the cards of your past at will ... so who I am is a lottery determined by me – I just have more numbers than most.' This means that she's free to pick and mix from all the characteristics on show around her. George Bernard Shaw was saying this very same thing when he said life is about 'creating yourself'.

Think of the freedom of being able to choose anything you want from what's on display, in whatever quantities. How liberating is that? You therefore now know that you don't have to turn into your eccentric aunt or madcap uncle – unless you want to, of course! You can turn into someone of your own choosing, turn out the way *you* want to. You get to choose your personality, design your character, mould your outlook, be whoever

> **You get to choose your personality, design your character.**

you want to be. Will it take effort? Definitely. Is it possible? Absolutely.

The more I hear about Warren Buffett, the more I like him. This seventy-something is the world's most successful investor – and one of the world's wealthiest people. In spring 1998 he co-hosted a fascinating discussion with Bill Gates at the University of Washington. The university's business students were eager to discover the secrets of these men's incredible success. Warren Buffett's responses were fascinating. He talked about habits, character and temperament; about the importance of behaving in a rational way and not getting in your own way. The one piece of advice he gave the students was this:

> Pick out the person in the class that you admire the most
> and then write down why you admire them. Put down a
> list of qualities and then put down the one that frankly
> you can stand the least in the whole group and put down
> the qualities that turn you off in that person. The qualities
> of the first one that you admire are qualities that you,
> with a little practice, can make your own and which if
> practised will become habit forming. The chains of habit
> are too light to be felt until they're too heavy to be broken

… you will have the habits twenty years from now that you decide to put into practice today. I suggest you look at the habits you admire in others or the behaviour you admire in others and make those your own habits, and that you look at what you really find somewhat reprehensible in others and just decide those are things you're not going to do. Ben Franklin did that a few hundred years ago and it still works today.

Groundbreaking research carried out at the University of California endorses Mr Buffett's advice. It shows that key aspects of our personalities – affecting everything from our stress levels to how spontaneous we are – are not set by the time we reach our twenties, as was once believed. University of California psychologist Sanjay Srivastava questioned 130,000 adults, with an average age of thirty-one, on the five key traits that form the basis of everyone's personalities – openness, conscientiousness, agreeableness, neuroticism and extroversion. 'We found that personality traits continue to change throughout early and middle adulthood,' Dr Srivastava explains. 'They're not set in stone like some theorists thought – they're like soft plaster. The idea that you can't teach an old dog new tricks is wrong.'

In other words, you can continually mould yourself into the person you want to be. Once you identify the personality traits and habits that are holding you back, you can take positive action to be the best you can be.

➤ Don't Be Typecast

It all sounds so easy, doesn't it? So what might make reinventing yourself difficult? The biggest obstacle you face at this point on your journey is this. You will have been labelled and branded from the time of your earliest memory. The extent to which you've bought into those labels – how deeply you're branded – is the extent to which you'll find discarding them easy or difficult. To an enormous extent, you are who you've been told you are. You are the label you're wearing, the brand name that was handed to you. You are loyal to them. You adhere to them. And you may not even know you're wearing them.

Make no mistake. You have been typecast. You have had roles assigned to you and labels slapped on you. You have been pigeonholed. In a nutshell, labelling is a self-fulfilling prophecy. More than that, labels box you in. Ironically, sometimes a 'positive' label can be just as damaging as a 'negative' one.

A friend of mine, Maria, has just abandoned her high-flying City finance career to follow her true loves, painting and interior design. She was labelled 'good at maths' at her convent school and steered towards a career in accountancy. Intrinsically, she is a really artistic person whose talent would have flourished at art college. 'I wish now I'd spent more time on art, but I felt I had to keep on the academic treadmill because it so defined the person I was,' says Maria. She's now building a profitable property business in London's trendy East End – using her eye for colour and flair for design to transform old properties into desirable homes, some of which she sells and others rents out. She feels she's on permanent holiday, loving every part of her day. It's taken ten years for her to discard the original label and rebrand herself.

➤ *Liberate Yourself*

Knowledge is power. Seeing the labels means you can unpick them. Understanding the branding positions you to review and update for a fresher, more 'now' look and feel. Remember, we're not talking appearances here. I'm getting to the heart of how you see yourself, where that identity has come from and how you can redesign yourself as you see fit. If life is one big, self-fulfilling prophecy, then whose prophecy are you fulfilling? Who foretold your potential? Who predicted your future? In other words, who still has power over you? Who's running the show here? What might be boxing you in?

You are putty in your own hands. Before we start sculpting the new you, let's chip away at the old you and discard what you don't want to include in the new mould.

➤ *What's Your Label?*

Let's now decide who you *don't* want to be – before we go into who you *do* want to be. You must pinpoint those deeply ingrained ideas you may have absorbed about yourself. Right now, make a list of five quality labels that you were given as you were growing up, real top-notch ones that you want to hang on to and make last for ever. These will be things like: 'is outgoing and sociable', 'is inventive', 'is original – comes up with great ideas', 'will go places'.

Now list the five labels that do absolutely nothing for you. These could be things like: 'tends to be lazy', 'is easily distracted', 'never follows through', 'is argumentative', 'prefers her own company', 'not a natural risk-taker', 'hard as nails', 'always late'. I've heard all of these from clients. Highlight those labels and see them for what they are – someone else's perspective and assessment. In fact, right from the outset they could even have been meaningless, throwaway comments that you grabbed onto and they sort of stuck ever since. These are the easiest labels to unpick or peel off because the minute you see them for what they are they practically drop off by themselves.

Have a close look at the labels. Is there any truth in them? Maybe there is. Maybe there isn't. Even if there is, if it no longer suits you to be loyal to a label, ditch it.

Take it off. Decide right now never to be true to it again. Place your loyalty elsewhere.

➤ *Rebrand Yourself*

If you were labelled as someone who 'doesn't like exercise' and this is no longer something you want to be true to, drop it now. It may have suited you not to run around a freezing football pitch in mid-November when you were thirteen, but that was then. Grown-up exercise is different. What label is more appropriate for you now? What do you want to be true for you now?

Do you want to be labelled as someone who 'loves exercise'? Go right ahead. That's a great prophecy to fulfil. It's your prerogative to do so. Now make it stick by adopting the habits and characteristics that accompany that label. Just copy someone who's a little ahead of you. It'll involve things like going to a great gym, having a training buddy, using a personal trainer, perhaps joining a running club and having favourite teachers and classes. And, of course, you'll get all the right gear so you'll be looking good from the start!

➤ *You Can Do It*

It really is possible to rid yourself of these labels, no matter how young you were when they were put on you, or if the labeller was an authority figure in your life.

Derek Beevor is one of the UK's smartest entrepreneurs. At forty-seven he has the tycoon's obligatory stately home and flies himself to meetings in his own helicopter. His company, Road Tech, employs eighty people and has sales of £5m a year. Derek is self-made from the very depths of his being. There was little indication when he was younger that his story would turn out so well. He left school with no qualifications after his teacher asked the class to write down what subjects they wanted to take for O-levels – but then tore up the list Derek had written and asked him to leave.

You can make your own guess at the labelling going on here. Derek ensured none of the labels dogged him or his life: 'When I left school I had zero expectations. I just expected to start at the bottom and work my way up. I always knew that I would have to make my own way in life and that nobody was just going to give it to me … you have to listen to your own drummer and not somebody else's.'

➤ *Don't Ask Permission*

Don't announce your rebranding to the world. There's no need to put out a press release. If you do it well enough, it'll show. Especially don't get hung up on trying to convince your original labellers and soothsayers that they were wrong about you. Forget about trying to hand back their out-of-date labels.

Concentrate your energy and focus on you. The labellers have had enough sway over you, knowingly or unknowingly, and now it's over. You're the one calling the shots now in the character and personality department. If they are so fixed on seeing you in a particular way that simply isn't true anymore, or maybe never was, so be it. Don't fight with other people. Your biggest battle is with yourself. You have no spare energy to spill. And looking contained and in control is really rather impressive anyway!

➤ *Who Do You Want to Be?*

You are the author of your own life. Only you can accept the accolades or take the blame if things go wrong. You are designing yourself anew every day; reinforcing qualities, hammering in habits. The question is not, 'Who am I?' but 'Who do I want to be?' This conversation takes you out of the box and into the realms of reinvention, because the truth is that you could be anyone.

> **The truth is that you could be anyone.**

THE WORK

1. Be Honest
What are your personality traits that do you no favours? What characteristics hamper your success in life, in every way? Ask a *really* good friend to give you an honest appraisal. All change begins with a decision. ➤

➤ Decide to alter direction right now. Steer yourself away from the course you were on to a more attractive place altogether. Be vigilant and get feedback.

2. Aspire Upwards

Follow Warren Buffett's advice. Identify the most impressive person you know. Make a list of the qualities they embody and the habits they follow. Study them. Make notes. Learn fast and learn well. Spend as much time around them as possible. Capture these qualities for yourself. Adopt each one for yourself. Begin to wear those characteristics yourself; weave them into your demeanour, character and personality. Weld them on to your persona. Soon enough you'll be impressing yourself!

3. Practise, Practise, Practise

Take every opportunity to practise your new persona. Get those new habits in place. Be real. Get them booked into your diary. They won't happen automatically or overnight – that's not the nature of habits. They need to be adopted and followed. If you want to be 'an exerciser', get those classes and runs built in to your diary. When you falter, get back into it again. Good habits are for life, not just for now. If you want to ➤

➤ be someone who's more outgoing, friendly and socially composed go for it. Accept a party invitation – or better still, have your own party! Practise your poise. See yourself in action. Don't make it difficult; a short, successful burst is far more productive than an entire evening. You can work up to it.

4. Choose Your Response

Your *response* to life is paramount. Get more conscious and conscientious about your choice of response. It's never ever what happens to you that has power over you – it's always how you allow it to affect you. You can also review the past from this perspective. Your response makes it one thing or another. Be rigorous with yourself in cultivating this habit. Stuck in a traffic jam? Choose your response. The wine bar is out of your favourite Chablis? Choose your response. It's raining on your wedding day? Choose your response (I appreciate that's a difficult one!). Build the habit of choosing your response when you face even the smallest challenges and you'll be in a better position to do the same with any big challenges that come along.

5. Talk Yourself Up

Reinforce the new you in words as well as in deeds. Ensure you are building on your current labels, not the out-of-date ones. It may feel like outright lies at first. Don't worry about that. It'll come true soon enough. Make your sayings and statements as close to the truth as possible; turning yourself from dithering to decisive may, for instance, require you to take the menu at dinner and say after a glance, 'I'll have the grilled turbot – no point in hanging about.'

Moral: Your vision of yourself and your life is your greatest asset.

3

Be authentic

Happiness is when what you think, what you say, and what you do are in harmony.

MAHATMA GANDHI

Life is so much easier when you know who you are. It sounds obvious, but do you know 'the real you'? Are you in regular contact? Do you feel connected? Are you authentic? How real are you?

There's something of the chameleon in all of us. It's hard to be a social animal without it and it's not necessarily a bad thing. We've all read '*How to make people like you in ninety seconds or less*' or '*How to make anyone fall in love with you*', or something similar. We all want to get along with others and to build social and professional networks. Successful socialisers have the knack of making others feel instantly at ease, establishing immediate rapport and a feeling of being on the same wavelength. Those who are *really* successful at this leave you feeling the most special person in the room.

But what happens to the real you in all of this? Could you identify yourself in a crowd? In all the busyness, could you get lost? Could you lose sight of the real you? Blending in could leave you feeling bland. Too much flexibility and suppleness will weaken your underlying structure. True strength and poise comes from a careful balance of strength and flexibility, from a strong centre. This is true for your body. It's called core stability. It's also true for your character. It's called personal integrity.

> **True strength and poise comes from a careful balance of strength and flexibility.**

Enduring reinvention is not about being a fake. Far from it. As a person of substance and some depth, that's not something you would find attractive. The shallow and superficial hold no appeal. Reinvention for you has to include attention to your underlying core, to involve your innermost depths.

There is no conflict here in my definition of reinvention. Of course you can adopt characteristics and habits to become the person you want to be. Being open to change is a prerequisite for an interesting life. However, the one solid, unwavering element about you must be your core values. You need to stay true to who you are at your core, however you alter the expression of those values.

Some of the world's most successful companies have successfully reinvented themselves while staying true to their original values. Virgin is a fascinating brand with core values of fun and anti-establishment. It can successfully spread its brand to extremes from travel to cosmetics, wedding dresses to Internet service provision. This is possible because whatever it decides to enter it still holds the same values throughout; there is no confusion about what it stands for because its core values are consistently upheld and conveyed, regardless of the item that is being sold.

When the once-staid Burberry revamped its image to be more cool, it employed Mario Testino to shoot Kate Moss and Stella Tennant for its ad campaign. The company's value rose from £200 million to £1 billion in three years. Burberry managed to widen its appeal to a new and younger audience, without alienating its existing customer base. The company stayed true to its traditional values as a solid, trustworthy, quality British company while extending the brand to be more democratic. Other companies have not been so successful. The Levi jeans company's values revolve around rebellion. In the 1980s, Levi decided to enter the suit market. This was a flop as it went against the very essence of the Levi brand.

Most companies today have a mission statement – a succinct description of what the company stands for, of its purpose. Mission statements have had a bad press for some time, and deservedly so. When companies use them merely as trendy marketing tools to appear to have values and a vision beyond pure profit, we can usually see through it. They're being 'fake real'.

But it would be a shame to dismiss the importance of a declared vision and a set of values to define ourselves and live by. A simple statement is invaluable as a quick reference point for our decisions and actions. We can easily see whether we are being congruent – acting in alignment with our personal principles and ethics. It's easier to be at peace with yourself when you're clear who you are and living a life that reflects and reinforces your core self. It's automatic to like and respect yourself as you uphold all that is dear to you. It's also invaluable in a crisis. When you are under fire, you will only vigorously defend yourself if you can *feel* innocent. Your conscience will be clear if you've been congruent, consistently upholding your values.

The good news is that you need never have an identity crisis. You'll never have to go looking for yourself in the desert or put yourself through expensive soul-searching retreats, unless you really want the break, of course. This is the time and the place to 'discover' and define the real you. If you're already clear, take this opportunity to review and reinforce yourself.

Who are you? Put simply, you are who you *say* you are. Your word is your bond. Your inspiration can come from spiritual or religious guides, but ultimately only you can keep your word. You get the final say. That's the beauty and the challenge of free will.

Like I say, life is easier when you know who you are. While you're defining yourself, why not go further still and divine yourself a Purpose? That's when life becomes really straightforward and, well, meaningful. Why not make your mission in life the fulfilling of your purpose, which also involves you staying true to an exciting set of values? That's irresistible. And you'll never do that existential angst thing of pondering the meaning of life late into the night ever again. You'll have figured it out, all on your own!

> **Life is easier when you know who you are.**

Knowing what the point of your life is gives it meaning. And living a meaningful life makes it important. There has to be a point, a purpose to it all, otherwise what's it all about? Day in, day out, your life could feel a tad mundane and, heaven forbid, humdrum. Frankly, that is not for you or for me. The meaning your life has is the meaning you give it. Here's a simple exercise that works. I've used it myself and with countless others. As the mystic poet Rumi said, 'Everyone has been called for some particular work, and the desire for that work has been put in their heart.'

Answer these simple questions with five words or a short statement for each:

1. What do you want most out of life?

2. What do you want to see happen in the world?

3. What makes you special?

4. What things can you do/are you capable of doing right now?

Now write this statement as follows:

I will … (Choose one answer from 4), using my … (answer from 3), to accomplish (answer from 2), and in so doing achieve … (answer 1).

Now you have a mission statement that gives you a purpose and strengthens your sense of self. Feel free to repeat this exercise on a regular basis to fine-tune and hone. But it shouldn't change that dramatically. How you translate this into your life is up to you, but why not infuse that ethos into everything you do? This instantly elevates even the most routine day into something more potent. Now let's get some values prioritised.

Your values represent your unique essence. They give your spirit its distinctive edge. To honour yourself is to uphold your values. Your values are already at work in your life. The more overt and explicit they are for you, the more powerful and useful they can be to you. Some values can take time to develop in life and will only emerge through circumstances.

Look into your life at crucial times of change. What values were you asserting when you made your choices? Check your peak moments – experiences that you found particularly satisfying and fulfilling.

Another way to identify values is to recognise what you feel you *must* have in your life. Beyond the physical necessities, what *must* you have in your life in order to feel fulfilled? Must you have adventure and excitement? Must you be moving towards a sense of accomplishment and unfolding potential? What are the values you absolutely must honour or part of you dies? Begin to compile a list as these values occur to you over the next few days. Some distinctions could be:

- Honesty
- Integrity
- Truthfulness
- Spirituality
- Harmony
- Personal power
- Contribution
- Lightness
- Joy
- Beauty
- Risk taking
- Peace
- Tradition
- Elegance
- Trust
- Independence
- Excellence

Add any of your own values to this list and rank the words in order of importance to identify your top values. Aim to have no more than five that are paramount. Look at how you live out those values in your daily life. How do you compromise them? What more could you do to be true to your values?

A note of caution. Guard against getting overly zealous in the execution of your values or imposing them on others. They're there for your benefit. Living a life of purpose makes life instantly more fulfilling. Ensure that the knock-on effect benefits everyone else. Then your contribution will be incalculable.

Once you know yourself inside out, you can recognise yourself anywhere. You can go anywhere without getting lost. You can mingle and mix with the best of them. You are also likely to be far less dependent on public approval than the average person. You don't need to consult a focus group before you express an opinion. You don't need a PR adviser to tell you what the popular mood is. You never need to sit on the fence, unless you're genuinely contemplating your position before making your move. This is a glorious place of personal freedom to aim for. Once you've arrived at it you'll know. The feeling of power, self-respect and liberation will be unmistakable.

You may court controversy, but that won't prevent you from being you. For generations this behaviour has been easier for men and actively encouraged in them. Nowadays there's nothing to stop women from doing the same, other than our own terror that assertiveness is unattractive and unfeminine.

Bridget Jones, the original heroine who dominated popular fiction for the past decade, is now gone. In place of the neurotic, chain-smoking singleton, Bridget's creator Helen Fielding has come up with a new heroine. Olivia Joules, her female spy, is, according to the press release, an all-action, ass-kicking, man-chewing heroine. 'Post-9/11, the idea of what a woman is has changed,' says her publicist. 'It's all about self-reliance, individualism and your own decisions.'

Before voicing an opinion on George Bush while performing at London's Shepherd's Bush Empire in March 2003, the Dixie Chicks were America's sweethearts. The Texan trio were chosen to sing the national anthem at the Superbowl two months before, they have sold twenty-five million albums and their album *Home* was at number one. Then, three days before America and

Britain went to war in Iraq, lead singer Natalie Maines said: 'Just so you know, we're ashamed that the president of the United States is from Texas. We do not want war.'

Public CD burnings and bans on forty-two country music stations followed, and they were branded 'Saddam's Angels'. Death threats against Natalie led to twenty-four-hour armed protection. In their initial shock at the backlash, Natalie issued a qualified apology to Bush. Since then, her resolve has hardened. One of the group's first public responses to the radio ban was to pose nude on the cover of *Entertainment Weekly* with slogans such as 'Traitors' and 'Saddam's Angels' superimposed on their bodies.

'It deserved a strong response from us and we felt it had to be in your face,' said Martie Maguire, a fellow Chick. 'The magazine wanted us standing in front of the American flag in our jeans and smiling for the cover. And we thought no. We had to hit them over the head with it ...' The third of the trio, Emily Robison, said, 'If you can't question your government then you are just mindless followers.'

Sometimes you have to go back to the past to create the future. Reclaiming your original spirit may be the key to a new life, and a fresh 'new' you. Sometimes the only way forwards is to retrace your steps and recapture the you that got left behind years before you gave in to the pressures of life and time, or just accommodated yourself too often, too much. Your spirit can get worn down over the years, but if you were feisty once, you can be feisty again and always. It's never too late to rediscover yourself.

> **Sometimes you have to go back to the past to create the future.**

Claire came to see me as a last resort. She had seen therapists and been on Prozac for a year. She felt she was wasting her life and her future looked empty. She was right on both counts. She was approaching forty and, though Scottish, had been living in Nice, France, for the past five years due to her husband's high-flying career. She'd done a great job of raising her children, but now aged thirteen and fifteen, they were increasingly independent. She had moved around Europe since she married, with much of her time and energy going into accommodating the requirements of her husband's career; this included making each move smooth and stress free for the family. She had moved around enough. Meanwhile, her husband was itching to move to Paris. This was the point at which she came to see me.

With her notes, Claire emailed me a photo of herself. I was quite shocked. Here was a beautiful, vivacious young woman, effortlessly stylish in that European way. I could see she was no wimp. Yet she was living like one. It was obvious that she had lost sight of who she really was, left herself behind during one of her many moves. Sure enough, when we spoke and I put this to her, she immediately agreed and gave me all the evidence I asked for to prove that she was a plucky girl through and through. Before giving up work she had held down impressive jobs in her native Glasgow and longed to be out in the world again as a player. That drive had never left her.

My work with Claire involved getting her back to

the person she had been about fifteen years previously, the real Claire. Over the weeks ahead, I continually challenged and pushed her to remember who she was and to behave accordingly. This meant standing up to her husband to assert that she and the children were happy and settled where they were, and that she would not contemplate another move at least until after they had finished school. Her husband accepted this.

Claire then enrolled on a fitness and personal training course along with nutrition, which she passed with flying colours. This was a true passion for her as she had relied on exercise to lift her depression over the years. She had experienced for herself its power to lift her mood and improve her self-esteem. She has set up a small, exquisitely arranged personal training consultancy right in the heart of Nice and also offers a shopping and styling service. Business is good. She's happy and the future is fabulous and unlimited.

Claire no longer lives the life of a wimp, but one of a beautiful, vivacious, plucky girl. She's simply being herself.

Cilla Black, one of Britain's most loved and highest paid entertainers, was interviewed recently in the *Sunday Times*. She lost her beloved husband Bobby four years ago at the age of fifty-seven. He was also her manager and had run her life since she was nineteen. Cilla has emerged as a much more 'out-there', extrovert individual than ever before.

When Bobby was alive, while Cilla wasn't working they lived a comfortable, quiet life in their home counties' mansion, 'It was waiting for the grandchildren. Fabulous.' Since her husband's death Cilla has realised that contented domesticity was more his style than hers. 'Bobby just preferred to be at home, with animals . . . he didn't like people, and I'm the opposite.' Now Cilla has her gang of loyal escorts and friends, known as the Syndicate, and is about to open a members' club in London's West End called – Blacks! The interviewer made a shrewd observation, 'She has not so much changed as reverted to what she was before marrying a homely sort and losing a bit of herself.'

➤ *Being Authentic*

'Being authentic' is almost impossible to pin down. Or is it? The quest for being authentic is today's alchemy. Self-assurance is the very first component. Add an irreverence for authority or hierarchy and an unaffected nonchalance for trying too hard. Don't try to be anything you aren't. Do your own thing. Be true to yourself. That way, you're always original. Let people discover you. You're real. You're authentic.

> **Don't try to be anything you aren't.
> Do your own thing.**

THE WORK

1. Develop a Personal Ethics Plan (PEP)
Write down your philosophy of life, focusing on what you want to be and do, and on the values and principles upon which these desires are based. Use the ➤

➤ information you've gleaned already about your mission, purpose and values to encapsulate it all into a tightly knit, practicable PEP.

2. Recognise Your Spirit

Look at yourself when you were eleven. What were you up to then? How did you express yourself, or try to? Your own unique spirit was evident then. Take a close look and decide if you need to nudge it more into your life and personality now. Never forget who you really are.

3. Your Word Is Your Law

Make and keep commitments and promises. Your integrity in meeting these provides the clearest demonstrations of your character and identity. Think twice about making arrangements. Only agree or sign up for what you have every intention of doing. Don't go along with stuff for a quiet life. Be who you say you are.

4. Work Your Purpose

Weave your declared, defined purpose into your every day. Don't wait for the Big Occasion or Gala, though these are undoubtedly plenty of fun and not to be ➤

➤ dismissed. Put everything you do into this meaningful context. Changing your perspective in this way could render your career relevant or clearly redundant.

5. Don't Get Pious

Don't get carried away with the righteousness of your mission. Stay light. Concentrate on being the living embodiment of your values rather than the dogmatic bearer and enforcer of them. Being true to yourself takes enough time. Convincing others of your position is not the objective.

Moral: Ultimately, authentic should be effortless. What you see is what you get. Be simple yet refined, unassuming yet mightily impressive.

4

What do you want?

Twenty years from now you will be more disappointed by the things that you didn't do than by the ones you did do. So throw off the bowlines. Sail away from the safe harbour. Catch the trade winds in your sails. Explore. Dream. Discover.

MARK TWAIN

Reinventing yourself has to have a point to it, otherwise why bother putting all that effort and time into cross-examining and challenging yourself? What's your point? The point has to be about your life itself. What you are undertaking is no intellectually detached enquiry, but a deeply personal quest.

What do you want? The choice is yours. It's also vast and greater for you than it was for your predecessors. Their lives were circumscribed by lack of choice, but we luxuriate in new freedoms. We change jobs at will, have children when it suits us, eat what we like and take holidays all over the globe. But what if the luxury of choice makes knowing what you really, really want actually more difficult? That is the question posed by Michael Wilmott and William Nelson of the Future Foundation, a consumer think-tank, in their new book *Complicated Lives*. 'Life seems more pressurised,' say the authors, 'because it is more complex.'

Is it any wonder that a simple question – What do you want? – is the one that most people dread? Yet the Sunday supplements are full of people who have asked this very question and answered it with a life change that is often brave and remarkable.

Middle-class families are leading the exodus from the urban rat race to greener, more relaxed pastures. Downshifting was first identified in 1994 by the New York-based Trends Research Unit as a widespread movement that was not politically or environmentally motivated. Now people were actually choosing, en masse, to earn less in order to do something more rewarding, or simply to have more time.

The gap year used to be the preserve of young people experiencing the world before college and work. But today's gap-year traveller is as likely to be a stressed-out executive or pensioner as an eighteen-year-old. Moreover these days a mid-life crisis can occur at any age. A new and growing breed of young corporate drop-out is emerging; these individuals are waving goodbye to their glittering careers in favour of a more meaningful life.

A recent report has dubbed the new generation Tireds – Thirty-something Independent Radical Educated Drop-outs. One of the report's authors, Howard Beale, said: 'A significant proportion of talented young people – precisely those who businesses are so keen on – are "protiring". Young people in a weird way have become older than their parents. The generation perceived to have it all are asking whether they want it all.'

Knowing what you want is easier when you know that all change begins on the inside.

Changing the way you perceive yourself may be the key to changing your life. I have worked with numerous corporate high-flyers who have been keen to break free of a way of life that they have outgrown. One of the stumbling blocks is that they have become 'institutionalised': they doubt their ability to survive outside the organisation. If the perks and pay are exceptional, it's known as the 'golden handcuffs'. They yearn to be more entrepreneurial, to be able to take more risks, and envy freelancers or people on the outside running their own businesses. Their greatest fear and worst-case scenario is that they don't have what it takes to leave and thrive.

> **Changing the way you perceive yourself may be the key to changing your life.**

At thirty-two, Paul seemed to have it all. He was a manager with one of the world's leading management consultancies and his future as a partner was assured. He was immensely valued and every inch the model employee. Sounds perfect. The problem was that Paul just didn't feel right. The long-hours' culture and client devotion meant that he had little time or energy left over for his wife and new baby, or for friends and hobbies. Nor did he feel he was really the company man they wanted him to be. One day he looked at a senior partner fifteen years older than he was who had everything Paul was supposed to want and realised he didn't actually want it that much. However much they paid him, he still felt robbed of the life he really wanted.

Paul came to see me full of anxiety and self-doubt about how he could provide for his family and make life work outside the firm. He felt he just didn't have what it took to design a freelance career. The greatest obstacle to his new life was his perception of himself. He couldn't have what he wanted because he couldn't imagine pulling it off himself. He was wrong on all counts. Paul had been a true maverick at university, speed-reading his way through his studies and playing cricket while everyone else sweated in the library. At that time, he had tremendous faith in himself, and felt invincible and instinctively optimistic. He had, however, adapted his mindset drastically to make corporate life work, and to build a career that was considered immensely successful. Now it was time to turn up the volume on the qualities he already possessed in order to make a different life work.

We listed the ways Paul needed to see himself, the qualities he needed to dust down and polish and a few new ones as well. He modelled himself on the coolest person he knew and identified the practical changes he could immediately start to make. Next we looked for the easiest possible escape route. Paul resigned, worked a three-month notice period and was immediately offered freelance work once news spread of his decision.

Six months later Paul is working a fraction of the time he used to work, for far more money and, with a friend, is setting up a small, very stylish, traditional gentleman's barber's salon in the financial area of London. If all goes well, there are plans for four more sites in other areas of London. He still has to work at shedding the habits of ten years of corporate conditioning, particularly saying yes to everything, working excessively and taking everything very seriously. He is, however, beginning to see himself in a fresh new light, as a relaxed, confident, upbeat character who has his own business, but isn't a workaholic, plays lots of cricket, and has his best ideas over a glass of wine and a decent dinner with friends. That's Paul – or at least it is now. It wasn't until he met up with one of his old work colleagues that he realised how far he'd come and that he really had made the break. He was free and *knew* he could handle it. There was no going back.

Your life is shaped by what you think you can or cannot do. Every person I've ever met has boundaries about life and themselves. The more expansive the person, the more expansive the life. The more restricted the boundaries – you guessed it – the more restricted the life. If something doesn't exist on your personal radar as possible for you, it's unlikely to happen. Life holds few surprises. Instead it tends to turn out much as we imagine it will.

We all have negative beliefs we buy into, most of which we don't know about because they are so deeply ingrained in our subconscious. Once you shake yourself as you've been doing, you wake up to their influence and are in a position to rethink yourself in a more ambitious way. Pay attention to what you think you can or cannot do. As Henry Ford said, 'Whether you think you can or cannot, you're usually right.'

Constructing a life based on your perceived limitations is not something I'd recommend or imagine you'd want. Catch your limiting thoughts as they pass by. Refuse to take them seriously or give in to them. They can only continue to mould how you see yourself and your life if you allow them to. Right now, ask yourself, 'What limiting thoughts have shaped and built my perspective of me and life?' Make a note of these thoughts and be conscientious about ending their reign of power and influence over you.

Deep and true changes come from the inside out, not the other way around. To break out of a life that confines you, you have to change your *perspective* on yourself. Shifting your *inner viewpoint* is what will really shift your world. I can push you, prod you, challenge

> **Deep and true changes come from the inside out, not the other way around.**

you to tap into your potential, but how far you go is ultimately determined by you and your viewpoint.

➤ *What's Your Perspective?*

Perspective is all. You are who you are and what you are not because of your past, but because of your perspective. Breathe deeply and take this in. To understand the power of your perspective is to begin to take command of your thoughts and your reality. Your perspective creates your thoughts and your thoughts create everything – and the way to control your thoughts is to change your perspective. Assume a different perspective and you will have a different thought about everything. In this way you will have learned to control your thoughts, and in the business of creating your life, controlled thought is everything.

If you imagined that the controlling and directing of your thoughts is a form of prayer, you would think only about good things, perfect outcomes. In other words, everything that is occurring and ever will occur is the outward physical manifestation of your innermost thoughts, choices, ideas and determinations regarding *who you are* and *who you choose to be*. It is your strongest thoughts, the ones you've held most fervently, that have constructed who you are now. Who you are in the future is up to you.

Pause for a moment and reflect on your perspective. Immediately you'll notice that you have a perspective on everything. You'll have your very own 'take', a view on you, who you are, what your future holds, everything. It's like a filter that you look through at life. It colours everything. All that matters is that you take command of that perspective and ensure it's pointing in the direction you want to be heading, the life you want to be living.

Joanna came to see me recently thinking that she'd never meet Mr Right. She was a glamorous, high-flying thirty-nine-year-old woman who had it all except the right man to share it with. Her perspective was that men always preferred younger, thinner women: that was just the way it was. Her perspective gave rise to an entire range of thoughts and determinations about herself. She convinced herself she was unattractive and dull. It was no wonder that her love life was in the doldrums. I realised that she had to radically change her perspective and her specific thoughts about herself to change her situation.

Firstly I challenged Joanna's overall perspective by pointing out all the evidence to disprove her perspective. I showed her example after example of gorgeous women over thirty-nine who had no problem attracting great men, often a lot younger. I flagged up Jerry Hall who, at forty-six, had just turned down a proposal of marriage from her millionaire lover – who is ten years her junior; Joan Collins and her new husband, sixty-nine to his thirty-eight, and on and on until her perspective shifted. Then we tackled her personal thoughts and beliefs. I pointed out situations and examples that demonstrated that she was actually downright captivating to men, that she was intrinsically very charismatic, with the look of a 1950s siren about her!

It took a number of sessions to redirect Joanna and change her perspective, thoughts and reality. This was absolutely essential, as she was on course for a really disappointing personal life. As soon as she really made the shift, she began to attract the attention of fabulous guys who thought her a wonderful creature. Nearly a year after that first session with her she's in a blissful relationship with – you guessed it – a younger man. Her perspective shifted radically to allow for this possibility.

➤ *What Do You Want?*

The challenge is to commit yourself to a way of life that really suits you. It begins with the question, what do you want? Ensure that your perspective of yourself allows for you to pull it off. Do the work on your psychology first. Establish who you need to be to live the life of your dreams and what characteristics you need to develop to achieve this goal. Do you need to be brave, resourceful, imaginative, cheerful, confident, relaxed and approachable?

THE WORK

1. What Do You Want?
You're reinventing yourself. Why? What will a polished, perfected version of you do that a tired, less self-   ➤

➤   assured you might not? What are your true aspirations, your big dreams? What do you really, really want? Acknowledging your aspirations is the first step. If you think you don't know what they are, let me assure you that you do. They may be a little under the surface, but keep looking and you'll find them.

2. Who Do You Need to Be?

To make changes, to bring about the life you want, what sort of person do you need to be? Which qualities need emphasising? Which ones need managing? Are there others that have to be whittled away altogether? If you're embarking on a freelance life, you'll need vast amounts of resilience, shed-loads of self-belief. You won't have time to weep over rejections, so be prepared just to accept them. As a confident, resourceful person, you're on to the next call, contact, pitch, meeting, whatever it takes to make it work. That's you.

3. What Are You Going to Do?

Once you know what you want and have aligned your perspective, you have to do something to make your dreams happen. The difference between thinkers and doers is what they do at this point. Revving up   ➤

➤ your psychology will only take you so far. The next step is doing something. Demonstrate your commitment to your desires and plans. Get busy. You know what you need to do, so just do it!

4. Rewire Your Mindset

Guard your every thought and word. If controlled thought is a form of prayer, what are you praying for? If your thoughts produce your reality, what thoughts do you need to subscribe to, fervently, unswervingly, passionately? Speak only of that which you wish to come to pass. Knowing what you do, there's no excuse for sloppy thinking.

5. Do Something Different

The essence of reinvention is change. Challenge the way you see yourself. You're not someone who sings in public, but you'd love to? Take lessons and sign up for a spot at the Open Mic evening at your local jazz club. Two left feet? Get outta here and take salsa classes. Mastering small, perceived limitations encourages you to take on bigger ones. Push against those boundaries. Give yourself more space and scope to manoeuvre in. It's all in the mind.

Moral: Your perspective creates your thoughts and your thoughts create everything. It is your strongest thoughts that have constructed who you are now. Who you are in the future is up to you.

5

Fake it!

To compose our character is our duty ... our great and glorious masterpiece is to live appropriately.

MICHEL DE MONTAIGNE (1533–92)

You may well be shocked by my advice to 'Fake It!' You could be wondering what part faking it has to play in true reinvention, especially as not long ago I was urging you to be authentic. I have regularly reassured you that this reinvention is neither shallow nor superficial. So, why fake it? Let me explain.

Right now you are poised on a fault-line between here and there – between how you were and how you will be. The challenge facing you is how to make the leap; how to get to the other side as swiftly and seamlessly as possible. You have studied your character and identified the improvements you want to make and the specific attributes you're ready to take on. Your dilemma is: how and when? The answer is: any time now is good. Once you've done the background work, it's time to act. There's no better time than right now.

How do you do this? The answer is: you experiment, you try it out, you rehearse. You practise until perfect. The more you practise, the quicker it becomes real, second nature, automatic. Soon enough you will reach the stage where you don't have to try so hard. It feels instinctive. New habits are installed through repetition. They may feel awkward, even difficult at first. Practised regularly enough, they'll kick in and feel entirely natural. At this point, you've landed. You've made the leap. You're well and truly integrated with the new, reconstructed you. You've arrived.

From the outset, your aspiration has been to personify the qualities and habits that you felt were most appropriate and attractive for you. You have set out to cultivate your character to be the living embodiment of all that you desired to be. You've thought about your life and seen the person you need to be to make certain alterations and improvements. Now is the time to think less and *be* more, to channel those aspirations into actions. Your world is shaped by how you think *and how you act*.

➤ *Your New Skin*

Taking on a new role for yourself, going from sour to sweet, intolerant to tolerant, mean to generous, will feel alien if you're not normally this way inclined. To make it work, you're going to have to play the part of the person you're stepping into. No amount of thinking can replace actually *being* the person you have in mind. There's only one way to get through this stage and that is to fake it. You have to *play the part* of your perfected self. You have to get under the skin of your enhanced character and inhabit the role.

If cheerfulness and friendliness are replacing impatience and disinterest, that switch requires a big change in your daily modus operandi. If this feels like an awesome task, plan to practise intensively for part of the day and ease off for another part. You'll also need to shadow and study cheerful, friendly people to model yourself on, to see how they do it. You have to demonstrate cheerfulness, to see yourself in action to know that's who you are. Otherwise it's just a concept. Conscientiously get into the mood before you leave home in the morning, and adjust as necessary as the day goes on. Slipping into the familiar and comfortable old ways could happen without you even noticing.

Don't feel the slightest bit hesitant about this approach. It works. It's not about being a fraud, but about deliberately cultivating your character. If you sit around waiting for these changes to slowly grow on you, it just won't happen. You have to do the work – and the work in front of you right now is simply to suspend your disbelief and jump: jump from here to there. The shell of the newly designed you is waiting for you to try it on for size. Jump into your new skin and bring it to life. You can make adjustments, and refine and smooth it once you're wearing it. Breathe and let it mould itself to you.

> **Jump into your new skin and bring it to life.**

Get under the skin and walk around being the new you, perhaps for a few days at a time at first to get used to it, but ultimately for ever.

➤ Behave 'As If'

The work here involves *behaving as if* you already possess your chosen qualities. Neuro-linguistic programming, or NLP as it is known, is a hugely popular psychological approach. It is the study of excellence, offering practical tools to achieve excellence in your own life. 'Behaving as if' is a big NLP term. Put simply, if you want to be more confident, you need to identify the recipe for confident behaviour. The 'ingredients' may include standing or sitting upright, moving in a relaxed, purposeful way and making eye contact with people. You will be doing the things a confident person does as they would do them, and will thus actually feel more confident yourself.

You could, for instance, walk into a smart restaurant and *behave as if* you expect to be warmly welcomed, offered a decent table and treated courteously, by ensuring that your posture reflects confidence and ease; have your shoulders back and down, and smile and make eye contact. The more you *behave as if* you are a confident person, the more confident you will begin to feel and become. By changing your behaviour, you are influencing your feelings. Organise your behaviour, and your feelings will join you later.

> **Organise your behaviour, and your feelings will join you later.**

I tried this out recently when I was hosting a large party and just didn't feel in the mood. What I really felt like doing was having a bath and an early night. This was just not an option. It was my party and people would begin to arrive in just over an hour. I lay in the bath and figured out how I would have to act in order to *behave as if* I was someone who was thrilled to be there; loving every minute of it, delighted to be meeting and greeting, making introductions, gliding gracefully from one group to the other, taking care of everyone.

Did it work? Better than I had imagined. At some point I had begun to *feel* that I was loving every minute of it. I was having too good a time to notice exactly when I began to think this way. In *behaving* precisely as I had figured a happy, confident hostess would, my feelings followed on. I just couldn't have opened the party waiting for them to put a smile on my face. Sometimes you can't wait for your mood to kick in to have a good time.

➤ *Attitude Is All*

Your mind and body are part of the same system. They influence each other. Your attitude controls your mind, and your mind delivers your body language. Attitudes set the quality and mood of your thoughts, your voice tone, your spoken words. Most importantly, they rule your facial and body language. Your body has a mind of its own, and is ruled by your attitude. Your attitude goes before you. It controls the quality and appearance of everything you do. Before you speak, it's obvious what you're thinking and feeling. No matter what you say, your attitude says it all.

> **No matter what you say, your attitude says it all.**

Walk into any shop or restaurant today and you can tell which employees want to be there and which ones do not. A cheery attitude or a chippy one? It's written all over them and you can even tell just by looking through the window. You're free to choose any attitude you like, any time. Regardless of the situation there are only two types of attitude to choose from: productive and unproductive. Choose a productive attitude to match the requirements of your situation, to bring about the outcome you're after. Of Jayne Mansfield, a co-star once said, 'She just walked out and assumed everyone would be interested in her, and therefore, we all were.' That's a productive attitude for you.

Having spent the early Eighties working in cocktail bars and restaurants in London, I know first-hand the value of a productive attitude. Even if it was your sixth shift in a row and the only thing you felt like doing was sleeping, once you were 'on the floor' the only way to earn tips was by having the right attitude. As if we needed proof of this, a team of scientists has just published a report showing that staff who bond with their customers could make up to 80 per cent more in tips than staff who don't. A study in the Netherlands observed staff in a fast-food restaurant who spent half their shift imitating customers' speech patterns, and half ignoring them. The tips rocketed when the staff copied customers' behaviour. Rick van Baaren, an assistant professor at Nijmegen University, believes this increase is all about bonding: 'If you mimic somebody, you effectively put them at ease very quickly, and create a bond with them ... they will treat you far better if you appear to be on the same wavelength as them. The key is to use phrases the person uses. Also try and act a little like them if you can. The empathy with you this creates is invaluable.'

Building rapport is another popular NLP theme. It's common sense when you think about it, but fascinating to see the phenomenal power of it scientifically tested like this. Successful salesmen and waitresses the world over practise this instinctively.

➤ Play Your Part

Good actors understand perfectly the power of stepping into a role. They know that to be believable and convincing in a role, they must immerse themselves entirely in the character they are playing. They *are* that character from the inside with their 'normal' self entirely concealed. To be believable they must look, sound and speak the language of the person they're playing. This is known as the 'method' school of acting, and actors often find it extremely difficult to shake off their adopted personas. They and their character have merged. They often have to studiously 'debrief' themselves to return to their original selves. Al Pacino said in a recent interview, 'I've been doing so many different characters, it's sometimes difficult to remember my own.'

I recently coached a barrister, Mike, who was keen to be promoted to QC (Queen's Counsel). We identified the attitude and actions of a successful QC. Mike said it involved a look of self-assurance, supreme confidence and an air of authority bordering on the flamboyant. Looking at himself critically he could see the shortfall. It was obvious he needed to talk himself up more and deliver his arguments much more forcefully, succinctly and compellingly in court. He needed to be much more decisive with clients and clerks, as befitted his position as the expert. Listening to others' opinions was one thing but people looked to him to be a confident leader. He saw he needed to speak up clearly and lead from the front much more often. Deliberating, dithering and delaying played no part in the make-up of a successful barrister and QC.

Mike monitored his behaviour carefully – both in and out of court – and gradually directed himself to be the charismatic, self-assured man his life and ambition needed him to be. He stands a much better chance of being appointed QC if he looks and acts like one.

➤ Faking It

Faking It is the title of one of the UK's most popular television series. Each programme features one brave person who is ready to take up the challenge to completely transform their identity. One of my favourites has been the purple-haired punk-band singer Chris, who, with no previous musical training of any sort, and without being able to read a single note of music, had to transform himself into an orchestral conductor in four weeks. He did so in front of the Royal Philharmonic Orchestra and 1,500 people, conducting in a competition with three other highly trained budding maestri, and impressing one judge so much that he put him at the top of his list to win. Another of my favourites was Spence, the former naval officer who pulled off the unbelievable coup of faking it so well as drag queen Britney Ferry that he's now hoping to become a full-time drag queen, earning £200 per appearance. 'I've found my calling,' says Spence. 'I know I can sing and I get a big applause at the end of each show, which is a buzz. I've become addicted to it … I think I need an agent.'

One of Steven Spielberg's recent successes was the film *Catch Me If You Can*. It is based on the true but incredible story of Frank Abagnale, Jnr, who financed a jet-setting lifestyle by conning banks, airlines and hotels out of $2.5 million, the equivalent of around $36 million – or £23 million today. By the time he was twenty-one, and without any qualifications, he had worked as a Pan-Am pilot, a doctor, a lawyer and a sociology professor.

Abagnale's first impersonation took place when he posed as his father's chauffeur to impress a bank; the second occurred when he moved to a new school and turned the tables on a pair of bullies. He carried on convincing others that he was who he said he was for another two years until the FBI caught up with him.

I am not about to encourage you to take to a life of crime, but Abagnale's story undeniably demonstrates the power of acting the part and behaving 'as if'.

➤ *Choose to Believe*

I believe that great achievers everywhere understand the importance of faking it. Leaders know the role of inspiring others to believe in the success of their endeavour, regardless of proof or actual circumstances.

Barbara Cassini is the person with the unenviable responsibility of leading London's bid for the 2012 Olympic Games. She is the woman who set up Go airlines in six months from scratch for British Airways, saw its value leap from £110 million to £374 million in a year and pocketed a reported £9.5 million when it was sold to easyJet.

Cassini knows that she has a job ahead of her to secure

London as the venue. Her response to a journalist's quizzing in a recent interview was most revealing when asked what chance she thought London had of winning the bid. Sixty-forty? Fifty-fifty? 'Oh, 100 per cent,' she declared. 'You have to say that. You have to come in every day and say, "We're going to win." Not in an arrogant way, but the way an athlete would prepare for the Olympics.' What a professional. Choosing to believe they can win is what will drive and inspire her team – and the rest of London. We'll be carried along with Cassini's conviction. Coming second, or losing to a better venue? Don't even think about it.

➤ Be Happy

The choice of who you want to be is yours. However, there is ample evidence to suggest that putting happiness at the top of your to-do list is a very good idea.

A cheerful disposition is definitely one to cultivate. Two of the world's most respected happiness psychologists have analysed more than 3,000 studies conducted worldwide since the Sixties. Professors Ed Diener of

Illinois University and Ruut Veenhoven of Erasmus University in Rotterdam have concluded that happier people are more popular and less prone to divorce, get ill less often, and lead longer and more productive lives than unhappy people.

In addition, a new study carried out by American researchers claims to be the first to prove a direct link between brain activity and immune function. Tests on volunteers showed that those who focused most intensely on bad times in their lives suffered weakened immune systems. In the study fifty-two individuals aged between fifty-seven and sixty were asked to recall two events – one that made them feel happy and another that left them feeling sad, fearful or angry. After the tests the volunteers were given shots of flu vaccine and their immune responses were assessed by measuring blood antibody levels.

The study found that the most intense negative thinkers had poorer immune reactions than other volunteers. US neuroscientist Dr Richard Davidson, who led the research, said, 'Emotions play an important role in modulating bodily systems that influence our health ... Individuals characterised by a more negative affective style mount a weaker immune response and may be at greater risk of illness.' In other words, negative thinking can make you ill.

I had to work very hard to make my own transition from rude, bad-tempered, intolerant pessimist to pleasant, friendly, non-judgemental optimist. It was a huge leap, and I occasionally lapse – but never to the extreme position that I once habitually adopted. A journalist recently commented that I was possibly 'the most positive person alive'. I smiled. If only she'd seen the unreconstructed me!

➤ Fake It

There is nothing insincere about behaving appropriately. Manners and etiquette codes have always taught the importance of conducting yourself appropriately as befits the occasion: your mood or inner feelings being considered quite irrelevant. Obviously there is little point in living a life that contains endless occasions and obligations that you dread. However, organising your attitude and composing your demeanour will carry you far, while your feelings can catch up. Your behaviour will nudge your feelings into line. *Acting* confident will grow on you. Soon enough, you'll feel it too.

THE WORK

1. You're Already Faking It!

Every time you've ever summoned up the energy to smile and make the best of a situation, you've been faking it. I'm just inviting you to embrace the concept wholeheartedly and use it more systematically. The moment you smile, regardless of how you feel, your entire physiology responds accordingly. Your very stomach expands, relaxes and secretes feel-good juices. The journalist Liz Hodgkinson has even written an entire book on the subject called *Smile Therapy*.

2. Act and Become

Think less and be more the person you want to be. Embody your new persona. Identify the walk, talk and look of your chosen character. The more you behave as if you are confident, cheerful, happy and optimistic, the more you'll feel it and become it. The positive feedback of others will reflect back the new you for you to see.

3. Keep Good Company

Hang out with people who are already what you want
to become. Generous, big-hearted, fun, witty and kind?
Go find these kinds of people. You'll learn from them
and their outlook will rub off on you.

4. Perform and Perfect

Making a major character shift can take time. Don't
panic if the world doesn't seem to be appreciating the
new you straight away. Keep on practising and you'll
be perfect soon enough. But why not have some fun
with this and set the scene for some light-hearted
faking? Take yourself into a chi-chi store – like a
Versace, Dolce & Gabanna or Prada. Behave as if you're
entirely comfortable, at ease and expecting no more
and no less a welcome than the next person.

5. Get Feedback

It's important to know how you're doing. You need
feedback. Are you being convincing? Are you walking
tall, purposeful, self-assured and relaxed, or whatever?
Unless you could record your every move on CCTV, you
won't really know. So, ask – turn to a smart friend and
ask them to tell you what you're conveying, ➤

➤ the sort of person you're portraying. It's essential for you to know. Even the greatest actors take directors' notes.

Moral: Everyone who got where they are had to begin where they were.

6

Look the part

Style is knowing who you are, what you want to say, and not giving a damn.

GORE VIDAL

True and enduring reinvention begins on the inside but shows on the outside. Once you decide to upgrade your inner self, you'll want to carry through the upgrade to your external appearance as well. You'll instinctively want to ensure that how you look reflects the new, updated you – it's essential to check that the internal you and its external expression are as one. Being comfortable in your new skin is the challenge here.

The look that you had at the outset of your reinvention may need updating. If you're shedding outdated attitudes and outlooks, it's very likely that you'll want to leave a few outfits behind as well. You may need a whole new look. A revamped you will need to reappraise everything – hair, make-up, grooming, the entire look of you. What you were saying about you before may not be what you want to say now.

➤ *What's the Message?*

I want you to think carefully about how your dress code needs to be in order to accurately reflect and reinforce the new you. Study your role models. Identify the look you need to have. There's nothing superficial about appearances. They speak volumes about who you are and how you see yourself. As you enhance and update your outlook and life, it's important to check that your appearance keeps up. Most people are unconscious about the signals they're giving out and the impression they're leaving behind.

There's nothing superficial about appearances.

I want you to get into the habit of consciously identifying the message you're conveying. Over the next seven days, before you leave the house, check yourself visually and label your look. What is it saying about you? If other people can see it, you should too. Without necessarily changing a thing, take a few days to cultivate this skill. Really good personal shoppers and stylists do this brilliantly. Look around you and spot other people's messages and labels. Observe how fitting the labels are to their aims and aspirations, or how unhelpful they may be.

This was brilliantly demonstrated to me recently when I took part in a radio discussion with the fashion writer Colin McDowell. To prove that we're always saying something with our outfits he assessed each of the guests sitting around the table. The interviewer, John, was deemed to be dressed ready to paint the garden shed. McDowell refused to comment on another guest at all, and I was apparently dressed for a party. Given that it was 10 o'clock in the morning, this was perhaps not the best possible look. A more restrained look is probably best for business. The appraisal really made me think about dressing appropriately.

It is best to adapt your style but concentrate on what feels right rather than continually trying to second-guess what might work. There are always individuals who cultivate their style and take it wherever they go, regardless of the occasion. Marlene Dietrich knew herself and maintained her striking individual look throughout her life: a swath of mink, masculine suits, high heels, red talons and those wonderful etched eyebrows. It suited her and it worked. She never compromised. That was her look and she wore it everywhere. Supermodel Kate Moss is never a fashion victim and always manages to look comfortable, stylish and entirely individual. The trick to achieving this effortlessly stylish look is to be consistent: avoid wearing a uniform of tracksuit bottoms, baggy jumpers and flat shoes at home while dressing up in totally different garb once you leave the house. It always shows. A sharp stylist could detect that this just wasn't your normal attire and describe your usual uniform waiting at home.

I worked with a client, Penny, on this very issue. She was a lovely young woman of thirty-six who had been married for seven years. She and her husband had a gorgeous cottage in the country and Penny was a keen gardener. The problem was that she felt

she traded glamour for comfort and that her woolly
cardigans and furry slippers were having a
detrimental effect on how she perceived herself –
and if she didn't see herself as 'a creature unlike any
other', how could her husband?

Penny needed to swing the emphasis from drudge to
diva. Out went the cardies, slippers and anything
else that smacked of matronly aunt and in came
furry mules, silk dressing gowns, beaded pashminas
and an elegant wrap dress. I insisted that no matter
how cold it got or how much gardening she did she
had to dress as a diva would in these conditions. It
is entirely possible to be cool and cosy without
giving up on style altogether. Turning up the central
heating was infinitely better than dressing like
Kathy Bates in *Misery*. We were aiming for Jessica
Lange in *The Postman Always Rings Twice*.

The crucial thing was to get Penny to really see herself
as an attractive, sensuous young woman. This simply
could not happen if she dressed as a frump for most of
the time, with her inner diva coming out only for special
occasions – and there was absolutely no reason why she
couldn't be a gardener and a goddess as well. So, dress

for yourself. What do you want to see reflected back when you look in the mirror? Who do you want others to see when they look at you? Do clothes help shape the way you see yourself? Absolutely. Can a slickly tailored suit help give you an inner glow of confidence? Definitely.

Sometimes a dramatic change to our bodies can alter our outlook on life and shake up our perception of ourselves. Going from a size 20 to a size 10 will provoke changes throughout your life, not just your body and wardrobe. I know people who've done this and the way they view themselves and the way they dress and present themselves changed dramatically. The way others see them and relate to them changed as well.

> **Sometimes a dramatic change to our bodies can alter our outlook on life.**

I believe that we embark on diets to improve our lives, not just our shape. Underneath that desire to lose weight is a more intense desire to get a better life. People often assume that a better life can only come once they've shed the excess weight, or they simply don't feel deserving of better things until they've accomplished that primary goal. I think it's no coincidence that a major weight loss is frequently accompanied by major life changes. I am convinced that people's motivation to improve their physical appearance is inextricably linked to a readiness to shake up their overall life.

Carol Vorderman has done this very thing. Currently the UK's highest paid entertainer, she has pulled off one of the most incredible and talked about reinventions in recent years. Her look has always been very mumsy, middle-aged and, well, frumpy. Anything but sexy. Over a period of twelve months she's shed not only 28 pounds from her body, but also nearly ten years from her looks. At forty-two she's found her confidence late in life, having dressed very conservatively until now. Nowadays you'll find her in raunchy Versace numbers by night and Juicy or Earl jeans by day and it's great to see her enjoying it. Her external transformation coincides with the end of her marriage, a new boyfriend and a move from the marital country mansion to a new penthouse apartment in central London. Which change came first we don't really know, but her new outward appearance certainly reflects her new lifestyle and our perception of her has changed dramatically. She is now being offered glamorous fashion and lifestyle shows as opposed to the daytime and home improvement shows the 'old' Carol used to do.

➤ *Appearance Matters*

In 1967, Professor Albert Mehrabian, currently professor emeritus of psychology at UCLA, carried out the most widely quoted study on communication. He identified three aspects of communication and his conclusions were startling:

- 55 per cent of what we respond to takes place visually.

- 38 per cent of what we respond to is the sound of communication.

- 7 per cent of what we respond to involves the actual words we use.

Over half of all communication is non-verbal. It is the look of the communication that has the most impact:

the way we act, dress, move, gesture and so on. Make sure you pay attention to your posture and body language. We all know that rounded shoulders look defensive and defeated and open body language looks comfortable and reassuring. Pilates, yoga and the Alexander technique are all great disciplines that can be used for improving your posture and leave you looking expansive, relaxed and elegant. Looking the part, dressing the part and the tone of our voice are what really convey our message.

Appearance does matter. Madonna, Kylie Minogue, Elizabeth Hurley, Lulu or any pop band in the world would all tell you that presentation matters. It's key to the overall package. Changing your public's perception of you requires you to update the whole look. Whether you're Tom Jones introducing yourself to a whole new youth market or part of a new girl or boy band, you'll need to figure out the look you need to project. Actors often say that they only really get into a part when they put on the clothes of the character they are playing. Their external appearance influences how they feel and see themselves on the inside.

Today, stylists are so prized and sought after that they have a status similar to the celebrities they style. Katie Grand has recently restyled Kylie Minogue, Madonna, Elizabeth Hurley and Demi Moore for the cover of her magazine *Pop*, and *she* is the one the papers are interviewing. No department store that wanted to be taken seriously would be without a good personal shopper to help you get the look.

➤ *What's the Dress Code?*

Decide what your dress code needs to be. It's your uniform, an essential part of your armoury, critical to your success. Looking the part is half the battle. When Madonna turned up to persuade director Alan Parker to give her the part of Eva Peron in *Evita*, she drew gasps as she swanned in. She *was* Eva Peron, head to toe. The resemblance was said to be uncanny, and she went on to be nominated for an Oscar for the part. Any performer I know who's serious about getting a role dresses the part for the audition. It makes it infinitely easier to feel what it's like to be that person.

What, then, is your role? What part are you playing? Be

absolutely clear. Your appearance speaks volumes. It is best to get it under your control and to say what you want it to say – to convey the right message about you. Dress the part or dress for the part you want. If you want to convince those in power of your intelligence and authority, dress to impress them. Skin, hair and hands deserve thoughtful grooming. It'll show. All work environments have dress codes. Ensure you've deciphered yours and are suitably attired. The flamboyant offices of Saatchi & Saatchi will be poles apart from City bankers Morgan Stanley.

> **Dress the part or dress for the part you want.**

➤ *Smarten up!*

'Dress down' Fridays, when office workers were encouraged to turn up in casual clothes, were introduced in some offices in Britain and the United States in the 1990s. It was argued that allowing employees to relax their dress code on the last day of the working week could pay dividends. Not so, according to a study for *American Corporate Trends Magazine*. For the study, companies were asked to monitor Fridays after allowing dressing down. They replied that they saw a 50 per cent drop in employees' commitment to the job, a 35 per cent rise in charges of tardiness and a 63 per cent increase in complaints by customers. In Britain, Richard Wilson, of the Institute of Directors, said, 'When you go to work and you have to wear a suit it encourages you to convey an image of professionalism and puts you in a different frame of mind. If you are rolling up to work in casual gear then it instils a more casual attitude.'

New York-based tailor Alan Flusser is the author of the recent best-selling style bible *Dressing the Man* and creator of the archetypal power look for the film *Wall Street* back in 1987. He is convinced that in tough economic times there is a greater need to look as though we're up to it: 'The suit has returned to its rightful place as the work uniform of choice … in times of economic difficulties, people return to traditional dress. Business gets tough so you have to look tougher to do business.' Don't overdo it is the message from Peter York, social commentator and author of *The Official Sloane Ranger Handbook*: 'Overdone looks overdone. Being properly dressed is not wrong, but overdo it and you don't add value, you end up taking it away.'

> **Overdo it and you don't add value, you end up taking it away.**

All the experts agree that women should opt for a well-tailored suit and the right heels for projecting an air of professionalism at work. They should also wear make-up. Those who do earn 25 per cent more than those who don't. In general, darker colours are more serious than paler ones and speak authority. Think black, navy and pinstripe, and remember the saying, 'Dress for the job you want, not the job you have'.

➤ *Get into Shape*

You know what to do. Get the look. It will be worth it. If you need to shed a stone or so to get it even better, get on with it. Don't underestimate the importance of feeling comfortable in your skin, with your size. Besides, it's important to exercise and have a strong, supple body that can carry you through life without breaking down. It may not be politically correct to say it, but there's just no denying it – a slim, fit body is important.

I grew up with a father who was a self-improvement fanatic. His ideas embraced physical fitness. We were the first and only people out 'jogging' around the streets of my home town, Lurgan, and my dad was pumping iron at Buster McShane's Gym way before it became a popular activity. He also maintained a year-round tan with ingenious positioning of a small, square sun lamp. He looked gorgeous! I'm all for pursuing the body beautiful and attaining your best possible look. Why not? You deserve no less. Just don't drive yourself crazy, as many people do, while you go about it. You'll get there.

British talk show host Graham Norton was interviewed recently and asked about the effect of his phenomenal success on his ego. He replied, 'Being thin and fit has affected my ego far more than success has.' How fascinating is that? He'd been plump throughout his life and was experiencing slimness for the first time, having recently secured the services of a personal trainer and shed nearly two stone.

Remember Kevin Spacey in *American Beauty*? Facing a mid-life crisis, he sets about changing his entire life. Setting up a makeshift gym in his garage and losing his paunch is part of the plan. When asked what he's up to his character replies, 'I just want to look good without my clothes.'

It's good to get into shape. You deserve to have the sensation of a lean, fit body that looks great – with or without your clothes.

➤ Get with It

Most importantly, dress for yourself. Present yourself as you wish to see yourself: strong, confident, going places and up to the minute without being a fashion victim. Decide on your look and then dress yourself accordingly. The days are long gone when looking sexy ended at thirty-five. Forty plus is no longer frumpy. Forty plus is Madonna, it is *Sex and the City*'s Kim Catrall, it is domestic goddess Nigella Lawson. We are no longer defined by age, but by attitude. And fashion is no longer an age-related thing. When it comes to dressing, what's age got to do with it? Nothing.

A recent Versace party in London's Victoria and Albert Museum had Madonna looking understated wearing trousers, a leather jacket and a high-necked blouse, with daughter Lourdes by her side. Her message was clearly: 'I'm a busy mum, and that's my priority.' At forty-four, Madonna's body is still worthy of a barely there Versace dress. Trudie Styler, on the other hand, left her children at home and flaunted her body with the sort of confidence that daily yoga confers.

Men too have the right to look and dress how they feel. Is Tom Jones still sexy at sixty? You bet he is to some people, as are Michael Douglas, Warren Beatty, Paul McCartney, Bill Clinton, Mick Jagger, Robert Redford, David Bowie and Paul Newman. What they all have in common is an ability to move with the times and look 'now', current, up to date, with it. Looking fashionable and youthful is available to anyone, at any age. Looking good, looking how you want to look, has never been easier.

> **Looking fashionable and youthful is available to anyone, at any age.**

Remember that you're the talent. You're your own calling card. Be your own best asset. Look the part. You're worth it so get with it.

➤ *Feel Good*

The most important thing in self-presentation is self-confidence. If you feel good, and feel that you look good and project that, then no matter what you are wearing other people will subconsciously agree. Conversely, no matter how fashionable or impeccably chic you are, if you feel awkward and inappropriate you'll come across as awkward and inappropriate. In other words if you think you look good, other people will too. Feeling attractive and sexy has far more to do with self-esteem than, well, anything else. Amanda Harlech is best known as Karl Lagerfeld's muse at Chanel, having previously fulfilled this role for John Galliano at the House of Dior. Put simply, she inspires the world's greatest fashion house. This is what she had to say in a recent interview on fashion: 'The only fashion no-no is hating yourself.'

Always remember: confidence is sexy. The right outfit

helps enormously, but it's confidence that you want to cultivate. If you feel confident and attractive, you'll radiate confidence and attractiveness. It's true what they say: 'You're as attractive as you feel.'

> **If you feel confident and attractive, you'll radiate confidence and attractiveness.**

➤ *Look the Part*

See yourself for what you want to be. Identify the look that suits you now, for both the daytime and evening, workdays and weekends. Don't be vague about what your appearance is saying. Pinpoint the message. If it doesn't suit you, change the outfit. Get 'on-message'. Speak the truth.

THE WORK

1. What's the Message?
Clarify what you want to project. Who are you dressing up as? What's the story? What's your part? How do ➤

➤ you want to be interpreted? Get conscious about what you're saying. Choose the look to match the message.

2. Question Everything

Examine your wardrobe for anything that no longer represents you. Less is more if you're left with clothes that feel right and true for you. Don't hesitate to let go of an out-of-date look. Who you are now needs representation. Examine your hair and make-up in the same enquiring light. Professional guidance costs nothing these days, so make use of it. Any decent department store offers a free styling service. Take advice.

3. Get Groomed

Whether you are a woman or man, rich or poor, make sure you look cared for. If you neglect yourself it could look as though life's getting on top of you, which is not a good look. Get the sharpest haircut, and the best hair colour you can afford. Manicures, facials and pedicures all add up to a high-maintenance person. Self-care is self-respect. Polish and preen yourself. Everyone else in the animal kingdom does.

4. Check the Details

The right accessories will seal your look. A timeless classic or this season's watch will complement your message. Keeping up with trends shows that you know which year it is and that you're in touch. A new bag or shoes from a current collection, whether designer label or high street, will do the job. Go for quality. It is better to have one cashmere sweater than twenty mere merino ones.

5. Feel Good

Work it! Psych up your confidence. You're as attractive as you feel and you're feeling good. Smile. Relax. Exude reassurance and bonhomie. Project composure. Have your shoulders back and down, your neck relaxed and long, your eyes ahead. Set these finishing touches to your look before you leave the house. Do the groundwork, put in the preparation, then forget about it all and just enjoy. Looking the part becomes second nature.

Moral: See yourself for what you want to be. Dress to fit the person you are and will be.

7

Move on!

Think wrongly, if you please, but in all cases think for yourself.

DORIS LESSING

Changing yourself and staying in the same place won't work. You embarked on reinvention for a good reason and your spirited self-revival deserves to be taken seriously. The final step in this process of transformation involves you examining your present in order to move on into your future. You've sought to upgrade yourself from the inside out. You've challenged your attitude of mind: reappraised values, updated your look. Now it's time to look at the way forwards.

Life is all about choices and priorities. As an alert,

switched-on person you already know that. Time and energy are both precious commodities and their deployment must be your number one priority. Moving ahead in your life with renewed vigour and clarity now requires you to reassess the practicalities. Who and what are you spending your time and energy on? Investing time and energy in a place or on people that you're out of sync with just doesn't make sense.

> **Investing time and energy in a place or on people that you're out of sync with just doesn't make sense.**

➤ A Fresh Start

It's essential to feel that you're living in the right place for you. If you've made changes to how you see yourself and you want to live differently, you might need to consider moving on. Nearly twenty years ago I lived a very counter-culture life in a large house with other like-minded people. Our house was more like a drop-in centre than a home, which I loved. Smoking 'herbal cigarettes' into the early hours was a great way to live until I decided it wasn't anymore.

As soon as I decided to be different, to give up the late-night lifestyle, I had to move on. Staying in the same place but being a different person just wouldn't have worked. I left an entire lifestyle and social world behind. I knew I couldn't take people from the old world into my new world. I found a new place to live and maintained one friend from my peer group. I also felt that I needed uninterrupted time and energy in which to figure out who the new me was going to be. I knew what and whom I didn't want. Figuring out the rest was the real challenge. You might not need to do anything so extreme – or on the other hand you might.

Changes on the inside push for expression on the outside. Transforming yourself and staying with the same people, in the same place, doing the same thing is unlikely to work. Either you will slip back and revert to form, or you'll create tension and struggle between you and the sameness, whatever it is relevant to – people, a town or the job you do.

Not everyone will like or approve of the new you. You

may feel out of step with people you previously spent time with. Or perhaps you will just need to expand your contacts to include some fresh faces and limit your exposure to the others. Enthusiasm is infectious. It'll rub off on you, so if you'd like more of it in your life, hang out with the right people. Negativity and apathy are equally infectious, so choose your influences. Peer pressure isn't just for teenagers. It's for all of us, for life. You're being continually influenced by the people you surround yourself with. They have terrific power to shape your outlook. Now that you've taken control of your own outlook and destiny, you need to ensure that the people around you share your vision.

This isn't about being judgemental. It's a wavelength thing. You've been fine-tuning yourself, adjusting your frequency. You've altered your position to a higher vibration of awareness. The position you used to occupy is vacant. You've moved on. It could mean that people who used to connect with you just don't anymore, because the distance between you is too great.

➤ *Don't Be Sentimental*

Change is good. Change is healthy. It's refreshing. It allows you to move with the times – the stages of your life. Staying put could well lead to stagnation, with no movement, no momentum and nothing happening. Trading up, moving on and getting what you want will not please everyone. You need to handle this, otherwise you'll hold yourself back from making the changes you feel inspired to make.

Obviously, you may have responsibilities and loved ones to consider, and consider them you must, but that need not mean abandoning your dreams and schemes. If you have children, they are of course the priority – but taking care of them and handling your own desires is not impossible. Make sure, however, that you don't use reinvention as an excuse to abdicate responsibilities. If you are a parent, then you already know that children must be taken care of first and foremost. Running away would never give you peace of mind, and you would unwittingly sabotage any attempts at a fresh start. A clean slate requires a clear conscience. Always remember your values and personal standards.

➤ *Run an Inventory*

Your moving on in life can highlight other people's lack of momentum. Their own frustration can look like logic to you, but it's only their own discomfort at your pumped-up enthusiasm. Enthusiasm can be irritating to people who feel resigned and frustrated. It's best not to argue with them or to try to justify your case. In fact, this is the very time to carry out an inventory of the people in your life. Who can stay? Who has to go?

Make two lists of the people in your life. Head one list Energisers, the other Drainers. You know which list people need to go on, so don't hold back. Include relatives in the lists. Get clear on the type of people you're hanging out with. Are they largely Energisers? They need to be. Be aware that as you change, someone who may once have been an Energiser for you may have become more of a Drainer. There will be a number of people who don't really affect you in any particular way – don't worry too much about them. Concentrate on avoiding the Drainers altogether or reducing your exposure to them dramatically.

➤ *Does the Name Fit?*

No discussion on reinvention would be complete without addressing your name. Does it fit? Does it resonate with who you are now? Are you comfortable being Doris, Mervyn, Ruby or Dean? There is absolutely no reason why you should stay with a name that you've been stuck with. Change it. Go from Tracy to Frankie, Pratt to Jones – whatever. I happen to love the name Fiona but if I was called by my confirmation name, Martina, it just wouldn't work. I'm a Fiona, never a Martina.

Is it any wonder Elton John dropped Reg Dwight or Sting dropped Gordon Sumner or Marie McLaughlin became Lulu? Denise van Outen sounds much more interesting than plain old Denise Outen. The Rolling Stones could never have had a bass player called William Perks. He *had* to become Bill Wyman. And Norma Jean Baker just *had* to become Marilyn Monroe. My dad was known as Tom in the south of Ireland where he came from, but used his middle name Michael when he moved up north. No one really knows why, but there must have been a reason.

> There's a lot in a name. If yours doesn't fit, get a better one.

So, there's a lot in a name. If yours doesn't fit, get a better one.

Be true to who you are now.

You may remember the harrowing story of the estate agent Stephanie Slater that made news around the world in 1992. Stephanie was kidnapped by a man posing as a buyer as she showed him around a property. For eight days she was held hostage in a box.

After her release Stephanie found settling back into her old life impossible. Alcohol became her way of blotting out the past. One day she realised she had to get a grip on herself: 'First I stopped drinking. Then I cut my hair and changed my style. I didn't feel like Stephanie any more – hadn't for a long time. The answer, I realised, was to leave her behind. "I'm changing my name," I announced one night. "From now on I'm Phoenix." I wasn't trying to deny what had happened, just distance myself from it. Once I could look back on it objectively, I felt able to get a job ... and started giving talks to the police about the victims of crime. Slowly life has come together.' Phoenix now lives by the sea on the Isle of Wight, a long way from her previous life.

➤ *How Do You Sound?*

Do you like your accent and the sound of your own voice? Does it travel well? At the age of ten or eleven, when I realised Northern Ireland would not be the place for my grown-up life, I decided to prepare for a more adventurous future there and then. The harsh northern accent had to go. It became a softer, more southern lilt, vaguely transatlantic, and difficult to pin down. In Northern Ireland it's known as a 'Malone Road' accent, after a very swanky area of Belfast. Certainly, I could go anywhere with it. It would travel with me. Many others before me have made that same decision and ended up in London, New York, Boston and Chicago. I left at twenty. A small village or a small country may be where you start out, but it's where you are going that counts.

I have, however, seen other people hang on to their accents, keen to emphasise their connection to their home country. My Aunt Joan emigrated from a small village in Ireland to California, yet forty years on she still spoke as though she had never left Kilmedy. Eventually she would return to Ireland to spend her final years there. Maybe that was the only place where she felt truly at home.

How you sound is important. How you speak could help decide how well you get on in the business world, according to a survey of British bosses. Directors of companies participating in the survey admitted to judging how successful, hard-working or even honest someone is by their accent. Almost half of British company directors believe speaking with a strong regional accent is a disadvantage in business, while only 7 per cent think it could be an advantage. As many as 57 per cent said they still see a businessman with a southern accent as more likely to be successful. Scots fared well: 43 per cent of the directors judged them likely to be successful, and they topped the list of businessmen who come across as hard-working and reliable or honest. A total of 47 per cent of those surveyed said they would see businessmen with an American accent as more successful than those with a British accent.

The reinvention of Catherine Zeta-Jones from a failing career in the United Kingdom to the highest paid British actress in Hollywood is well known. However, her determination to take herself to the top also involved a deliberate decision to alter her accent to further her career. The Swansea-born actress's lilting Welsh tones have softened into more of a London/New York drawl.

As an ambitious young actress keen to make it, losing her native accent was a necessity in Hollywood. 'It was really difficult because I had a British-Welsh accent and there aren't so many British-Welsh roles. I needed an American accent for more opportunities to come my way. I had no work in Britain and came to the States wondering what the hell I was doing, joining the big line of pretty girls wanting to be actresses.' Reinventing herself had to include reinventing her voice.

Go right ahead and choose a voice that you find pleasing and that expresses who you are. Take no notice of detractors. It's your voice after all.

➤ *The Comeback*

F. Scott Fitzgerald said there are no second acts in American lives. It's the most untrue thing ever. There are second and third and fourth acts. Thirty years ago Tatum O'Neal was the youngest performer in movie history to win an Oscar, for *Paper Moon*. Her career declined because of cocaine and heroin addiction, and her disastrous marriage to tennis star John McEnroe ended in an acrimonious divorce. At the age of forty, things are now looking up for Tatum. She's reconciled with her leukaemia-stricken father, actor Ryan O'Neal, and has won excellent reviews for her performances in two films, *The Scoundrel's Wife* and *The Technical Writer*.

America embraces honest reinventions. They'll even take in fallen stars from other places. Sarah Ferguson, formerly HRH The Duchess of York, was divorced and bankrupt and had her royal title stripped from her when she headed to the United States. America embraced her. There, Fergie is an icon, the very model of someone who has gone from riches to rags to riches again. As the spokesperson for Weight Watchers in America, she is routinely applauded as she comes on stage to the tune of 'I will survive'. Over there they adore her. I can't think of another British celebrity who has quite pulled off such a dramatic reinvention as she has. It's hard to imagine her transforming herself like this in Britain. She needed to start afresh somewhere else and return remade.

➤ *Move On*

You are redefining your destiny as you decide on your future. Who you are and will become is down to you. Moving on may not win everyone's approval, but that was never part of the plan. Don't compromise yourself. <u>You are all you've got</u>. The future is ahead of you. When the time is right, move on.

> **Who you are and will become is down to you.**

THE WORK

1. Liberate Yourself

Don't hoard. Resist clinging on to the past with boxes of mementoes and photographs. I'm not saying erase the past; just pare down the space it occupies in your home and in your head. Be selective about your memories. Go through those boxes and refine what's really important and worth keeping. It goes without saying that this ➤

➤ principle should be applied regularly to all parts of your environs and life. Love the past, but stand square in your present and future.

2. Learn to Say No

In order to bring in the new you need to make space for new people, new pursuits and perhaps even a whole new life. Saying 'Yes' to these new things means saying 'No' to the stale, outdated things. These may be habits, attitudes, people or places. It is up to you to decide.

3. Be Responsible

The process of redefining yourself confirms your personal identity, worth and authentic power. You must now, more than ever, assume 100 per cent responsibility for the quality of your life. You are decisive and self-directed, knowing there is no one else to blame for not getting what you want out of life. Make the choice to be happy, more fun loving, spontaneous or whatever. Then ask yourself what you need to do to achieve these things.

4. Shake Yourself

Fall in love with change, both minor and major. Take a vegan cookery course; take lessons and get your Institute of Advanced Motorists badge; become an expert in flower arranging or basic car maintenance; qualify as an astrologer or nutritionist, or whatever fascinates you. With the major changes, check whether you're still happy living where and how you do. Be honest. What or who needs to go?

5. Choose Your Peer Pressure

It may be easier to let people go than you think. If you just stopped feeding your friendship with them with calls, cards and dinners, it could just fall by the wayside quite naturally. Try it. With other people, you may have to be a bit firmer. It's essential to have the right people around you to reinforce the New You.

Moral: Learn to stand alone, secure in your own Integrity and self-worth.

➤ *And Finally*

Well done for getting this far. You've stayed the course. You're no ordinary person. You're one of life's great initiators, shaping your destiny and moulding your life so it honours and reflects your highest potential. You are continually expanding your vision of what's possible, and life fits around you.

Be optimistic. Keep on telling yourself that you are dynamic, clever, likeable or whatever and you will behave in a way that fulfils this belief. Never forget that ways of thinking and thus behaving are simply habits. It takes about twenty-one conscious attempts to change a way of thinking and behaving to form new neurological pathways in the brain, and for these new ways to become a habit. Stick with it. Then, one day, you'll catch sight of yourself and think, 'My, is that me? Aren't I looking good?'

Absolutely!

FIONA HARROLD

Fiona Harrold's earliest exposure to coaching was at the age of eleven when, growing up in Northern Ireland, her beloved father would inspire her with the likes of Norman Vincent Peale, Napoleon Hill and Dale Carnegie – the US founding fathers of twentieth-century self-help philosophy. Michael Harrold was a charismatic individual who breathed fire into her sense of herself, implanting the belief that she could do anything. This is precisely what she does for her clients – among them many high-profile figures from the worlds of politics, entertainment and the media. She also provides ongoing coaching and consulting to a number of businesses, and has recently set up the first volunteer coaching programme for teenagers in a London school with plans to extend the programme nationwide.

Fiona's special passion is to make the world a better place to live by helping people discover and develop their own unique qualities and talents. Her intention is to take the principles of personal responsibility, individual self-help and mutual support to the widest public through The Next Level Club, and its wide range of motivational services and courses. Her website receives in excess of 500,000 visitors each month.

Fiona has over 15 year's experience coaching people from all walks of life. She is the author of the best-selling *Be Your Own Life Coach* (Hodder Mobius), *The 10-Minute Life Coach* (Hodder Mobius). Her next book for Piatkus, *Indestructible Self-belief*, will be published in late 2004.

Fiona makes frequent TV appearances and features regularly in the UK media, with columns in *Eve, Slimming* and *More!* magazines. She is based in London.

To receive Fiona's free weekly Newsletter, join The Next Level Club, or contact a FHC Coach, please visit www.fionaharrold.com.

THE NEXT LEVEL CLUB

'Cherie Blair has one, Madonna has one; now you too can afford your own life coach'

UK's top life coach offers everyone the chance to change their lives:

Background

Millions of people want to change their lives. One recent study showed that over half of respondents would like to change their lives but never seemed to find the time, whilst nearly a quarter admitted that they would be too afraid.

We may have more opportunities and freedom than any other generation, but too many choices and too many demands can also leave people feeling burned out and unsatisfied. The pressure is on as never before to fulfill our potential and live the best life possible. The challenge we face today is to grasp this freedom and design a life that really works.

Life coaching for everyone

This is exactly why the UK's leading life coach, **Fiona**

Harrold, is launching **The Next Level Club.** The Club is in response to the many requests she has received from readers of her best-selling books, *Be Your Own Life Coach* and *The 10-Minute Life Coach*.

Fiona says, 'To be a success at anything in life you need high levels of self-confidence and the right people behind you. The Next Level Club's combination of expert coaches and the camaraderie of like-minded people will guarantee that you feel able to achieve anything you really want and put your mind to.'

What is life coaching?
'Life coaching is not the same as having someone who tells you what to wear or how to apply your lipstick. It's about having someone behind you giving you the confidence and the self-belief that you can have the life you have always dreamed of.

'You might be a high-flying lawyer who has a passion for cooking and has always dreamed of opening a restaurant. You might be a stay-at-home mum who thinks she no longer has what it takes to get back into the job market. You might be a taxi-driver in Manchester whose secret desire to own a fishing boat and live in Cornwall.

And each of you is thinking "I can't do that because …". Life coaching is all about giving you the confidence to make it happen for yourself.'

Launch of The Next Level Club
The Next Level Club launches in central London in the spring of 2004 and will be nationwide by the end of the year. Week by week members will be coached to aim high and take decisive action to achieve and live their dreams. Membership of the Club is open to everyone.

'The Next Level philosophy is about taking total responsibility, overcoming barriers and supporting people as they live their dreams on a day-to-day basis. No psychobabble, no pampering, just inspirational coaching and down-to-earth strategies to get you to where you want to be.

'Whether you want to reinvent yourself, redesign your career, improve your dating confidence or simply work less and earn more The Next Level Club is the place to come to make it happen.'

You can find out how to join the Next Level Club at www.fionaharrold.com.